CONTENTS

Introduction

Chapter One
Chipping Away   6

Chapter Two
Robo-roach   16

Chapter Three
Make Way for Segway   26

Chapter Four
Flying Solo   34

Glossary   44

Find Out More   46

Index   47

DISCARDED

1002057

High-tech Inventions

A CHAPTER BOOK

BY MAR

High-Tech Inventions

Mary Packard

Lex: 770   RL: 4.3   GRL: P   Pts: 3

High-tech inventions :
609 PAC

1002057

Packard, Mary.

Fraser Valley Elementary

childre

A Division
New York   Toronto
Mexico City   N
Danbury, Connecticut

For Justin and Kate

ACKNOWLEDGMENTS

The author would like to thank all those who gave their time and
knowledge to help with this book. In particular, special thanks go to
David Weil, Executive Director of the Computer Museum of America,
Carla M. Vallone, Communication Manager for Segway LLC,
Robert Bulaga, and Warren G. Wettenstein,
Vice President of Trek Aerospace, Inc.

Library of Congress Cataloging-in-Publication Data

Packard, Mary.
  High-tech inventions : a chapter book / By Mary Packard.
    p. cm. – (True tales)
  ISBN 0-516-23728-4 (lib. bdg.)   0-516-24684-4 (pbk.)
  1. Computers—History—Juvenile literature. I. Title. II. Series.
  QA76.23.P33 2004
  004–dc22

                      2004000424

© 2004 Nancy Hall, Inc.
Published in 2004 by Children's Press, an imprint of Scholastic Library Publishing.
All rights reserved. Published simultaneously in Canada.
Printed in China.

CHILDREN'S PRESS and associated logos are trademarks and or registered trademarks
of Scholastic Library Publishing. SCHOLASTIC and associated logos are trademarks and
or registered trademarks of Scholastic Inc.

3 4 5 6 7 8 9 10 R 13 12 11 10 09 08
                                    62

INTRODUCTION

Imagine a computer so tiny it fits in your hand, a live insect whose movements you control, a scooter that can practically run itself, and a one-person flying machine. These things might seem impossible, but they have all been invented.

ENIAC, the first modern computer, was so big it took up an entire room. Jack Kilby and Robert Noyce's invention of the **integrated circuit** allowed computers to become much smaller. Isao Shimoyama has created a cockroach that is part insect and part machine. His invention, Robo-roach, will one day be able to explore spaces too tiny for humans. Dean Kamen invented a scooter that is steered by a rider's body movements. Michael Moshier dreamed of flying like a bird. That's why he's developing his own personal flying machine.

Read the stories behind these **high-tech** inventions. Who knows? Maybe someday you will get an idea for a high-tech invention of your own.

CHAPTER ONE

CHIPPING AWAY

Jack Kilby and Robert Noyce did not know
each other. They worked in companies that
were many miles apart. Yet in 1958, the two
scientists invented the same thing—the
integrated circuit, or IC. Their invention
was less than an inch long, but it changed
the world. With the IC, computers could be
made small enough for everyone to use.

Robert Noyce

Jack Kilby

Integrated circuit board

ENIAC took about a year to design and eighteen months to build.

Computers did not always fit on desks or on laps. At one time they were so large they filled entire rooms. What happened to make them shrink? The story of the modern computer began in Philadelphia. In 1945, the city's bright lights began to flicker and go dim. People were puzzled. What could be causing this?

The answer turned out to be ENIAC, the world's first electronic computer. A monster of a machine, ENIAC took up a whole room in the University of Pennsylvania. It weighed 30 tons, as much as a large truck. When the computer was working, it got so red-hot it glowed. Hundreds of lights blinked on and off.

What kind of work did ENIAC do? It added, subtracted, multiplied, and divided. It did these jobs very, very quickly. ENIAC solved difficult math problems in seconds, the same problems it took people days to figure out.

The trouble with ENIAC was that it used too much electricity. That's because it needed 18,000 vacuum tubes. Vacuum tubes are glass tubes with wires inside. They make electricity flow in one direction at a time. Each tube acts like a switch that can be turned on or off.

Vacuum tube

It took up to two days to reprogram ENIAC.

Vacuum tubes used so much electricity that they often overheated and stopped working. With ENIAC, at least fifty vacuum tubes had to be replaced each day.

Then, in 1947, a new kind of electronic switch was invented. It was called the **transistor**. The transistor took up less space than a vacuum tube. It used a much smaller amount of electricity, too. A vacuum tube is about the size of an adult's thumb. Fifty transistors take up the same amount of space as one vacuum tube.

Transistors act like on and off switches, just as vacuum tubes do. However, they use much less electricity. Since transistors don't need much power, they don't get hot. That is why they last such a long time.

With transistors, a computer could be built with a million switches. Complicated math problems could be solved even faster. Also, a computer with a million transistors would take up less room than ENIAC and use less electricity.

Transistors

11

It was hard to build this kind of computer. The problem was wires. The wires on a million transistors would have to be connected by hand. It would be almost impossible for people to put together all those parts without making any mistakes. Also, it would take a very long time.

Scientists needed to find another way to join the transistors. Scientists Jack Kilby and Robert Noyce had the same idea at nearly the same time. They came up with a way to combine many transistors into one **unit**. For Jack, that unit was a piece of **germanium** (jer-MAY-nee-um). For Robert, it was a piece of **silicon**.

Computer wires

With Jack and Robert's invention of the IC, it became possible to shrink a 30-ton computer down to the size of a refrigerator. Compared to ENIAC, that was tiny.

Jack Kilby's notebook and two original integrated circuits

Over the years, ICs became smaller and smaller. Today, thirty-five million transistors can fit on one flake of silicon! In order to see an IC chip clearly, you would need a microscope.

As ICs shrank, so did computers. Today, computers can be built to fit on a desk, on a lap, or even in the palm of your hand!

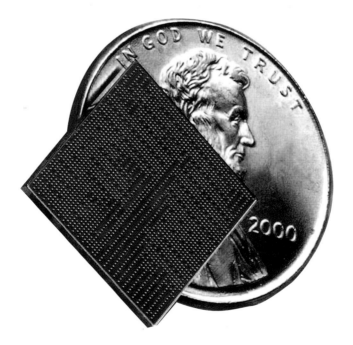

This IC chip is smaller than a penny.

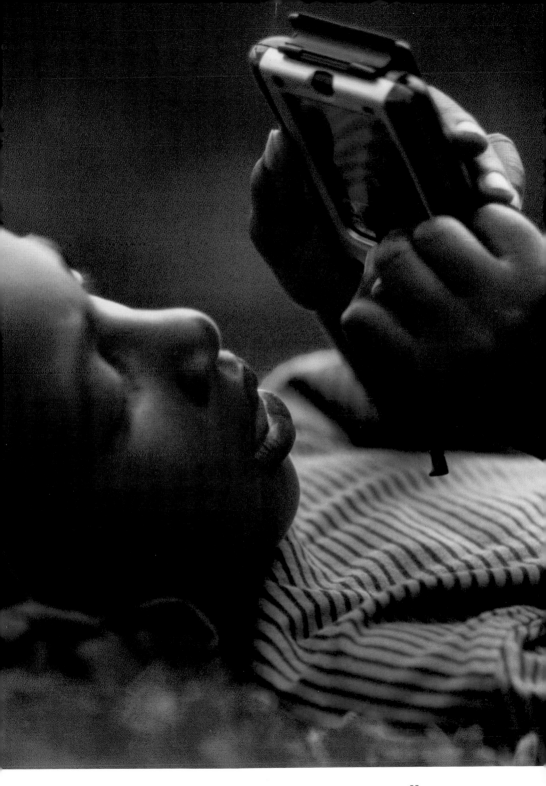

Now that so many computers are small,
they can be used anywhere.

CHAPTER TWO

ROBO-ROACH

Professor Isao Shimoyama and a team of scientists were in a laboratory at the University of Tokyo in Japan. Isao pressed a button on a remote control. A live cockroach backed up. He pressed another button. The cockroach moved forward. The next button made the cockroach turn right. What was going on?

Isao Shimoyama

Robo-roach

Isao was trying out Robo-roach, his new invention. By pressing different buttons on the remote, he could control the insect's movements. This cockroach was not just any bug. It was a **cyborg**. A cyborg combines a living being with manmade parts. Isao and his team of scientists started working on Robo-roach in the 1990s. It took them many years to make it work.

This man has a mechanical hand, which he uses to play the piano.

Before the scientists could create a cyborg like Robo-roach, two things had to happen. First, wireless **technology** (tek-NAH-luh-jee) had to be invented. Wireless technology makes it possible to send electrical messages without wires. If you turn on the radio or chat on a cell phone, you are using wireless technology. Next, integrated circuit chips

Cell phone

Radio

had to become small enough to fit on the back of an insect.

Once these inventions were in place, it was time to experiment. Isao chose to work with cockroaches because they are easy to find. In fact, roaches are one of the most common insects in the world. They have

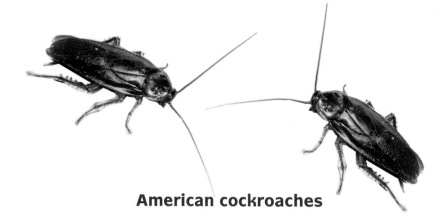

American cockroaches

been around longer than dinosaurs.
They have survived the **Ice Age**, floods,
and earthquakes.

Like all insects, cockroaches find their
way around by using their **antennae** (an-
TEN-ee). If a cockroach comes up against
an **obstacle** (OB-stih-kuhl), its antennae
will rub against it. When that happens, a
message is sent down the antennae and into
the roach's brain. The message tells the
cockroach that there is something in its way.

To create his cyborg, Isao used the
American cockroach. This **hardy** creature
can carry twenty times its own weight.
Before Professor Isao began work on the
cockroach, he connected a tiny computer

chip to a pair of **electrodes**. An electrode is a special wire that carries an electrical message. Then, Isao selected the biggest roach he could find.

After putting the roach to sleep with gas, Isao removed its wings and antennae.

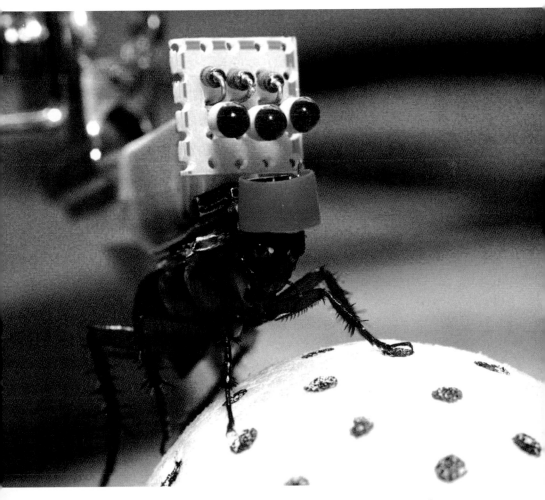

Robo-roach wearing a high-tech backpack

Isao Shimoyama holding Robo-roach and the remote control

He fitted the computer chip into a tiny backpack and attached it to the roach's back. Then he connected each electrode to where the antennae used to be.

After the cockroach woke, Isao and the other scientists picked up the remote control. Pressing a button sent a message to the computer chip in Robo-roach's backpack. This caused the computer chip to send a signal to an electrode. When the signal reached Robo-roach's brain, the brain followed the command. For instance, if the message was delivered to the left electrode, Robo-roach's brain would have information that an obstacle was on the left and it needed to turn right.

The placement of the electrodes is important. If they are not put into exactly the right place in the brain, the cyborg might not do what it is asked. Instead of making a turn, it might race off the table.

After several months, the cockroach becomes less **sensitive** to the electrical messages it gets from the computer chip. Isao and his team of scientists are looking for ways to make Robo-roach last longer.

After this problem has been solved, Isao plans to fit Robo-roach with tiny microphones and cameras. Then Robo-roach might be used to go on search and rescue missions. It could go into caves to find trapped miners. It could crawl through **rubble** to find people who have survived earthquakes.

These are just a few of the ways Robo-roach might help people. Can you think of other ways?

One day, remote-controlled insects could
help find people buried under rubble.

CHAPTER THREE

MAKE WAY FOR SEGWAY

Charles Gibson stepped onto a two-wheeled scooter. As the host of a television news show, Charles was about to test drive Dean Kamen's invention, the Segway HT (Human Transporter). The Segway HT doesn't have a steering wheel. How would Charles make the scooter go in the direction he wanted it to go?

Dean Kamen

Dean Kamen on his invention, the Segway HT

As Charles found out, all he had to do was lean. If he leaned forward, the scooter went forward. If he leaned to the right, the scooter turned right. If he leaned to the left, the scooter turned left.

The Segway HT is Dean Kamen's newest invention. He has had many others. His water purifier will provide clean drinking water for people living in poor countries. His wheelchair that climbs stairs will improve the lives of people who are unable to walk. Dean knows that science can change people's lives.

Dean's wheelchair invention can climb stairs.

Traffic contributes to air pollution.

Dean's home is in the hills above Manchester, New Hampshire. The air is clean there, and the water is pure. Dean would like for everybody to live in a clean **environment**. The Segway HT is Dean's answer to the problem of air **pollution**. Air can get polluted in many ways. One way is when too many cars are on the road at one time. That's because car **engines** burn gasoline. The **exhaust** (eg-ZAWST) that is left over comes out the back of cars in puffs of smoke. Exhaust makes the air dirty and bad to breathe.

This mail carrier uses the Segway HT to deliver mail.

Of course, the Segway HT is not meant to replace the car completely. As Dean says, "Cars are great for going long distances." Instead, he sees people using his invention in parks, on busy city streets and sidewalks, and even in factory warehouses. Driving a car would be impractical in these kinds of places.

The Segway HT's motors run on batteries. The scooter doesn't need gasoline, so it doesn't have a gas pedal, an exhaust pipe, or brakes. It can travel as fast as 12.5 miles (20 kilometers) per hour. It doesn't cost much to use, either. Even if you drive it all day, you will use only five or ten cents worth of electricity.

To ride the scooter, you stand on a small **platform**. Inside the platform are five **gyroscopes** (JYE-ruh-skopes). A gyroscope is a spinning wheel inside a frame. It keeps its position no matter in which direction it is moved. The gyroscopes keep the scooter balanced, not falling forward or tipping to the side.

Gyroscope

To go forward, a rider leans forward. Ten mini-computers in the scooter sense the movement of the rider through information given to it by the gyroscopes. The mini-computers direct the motors to turn the wheels forward. The more the rider leans forward, the faster the wheels turn. When the rider no longer leans forward, the scooter stops moving.

To go left and right, the rider turns a grip on the left side of the handle bars. To go left, the rider twists the handle left. To go right, the rider twists it right.

Imagine if every city dweller had a Segway HT to ride to work. The air would be much cleaner and safer to breathe. This might happen in the future. Dean Kamen believes that the Segway HT "will be to the car what the car was to the horse and buggy."

In the future, many people might use Segway HTs.

FLYING SOLO

In December 2001, Michael Moshier strapped himself into his own personal flying machine. As Michael stood in his company's parking lot, two fan blades above his head began to spin. Would he take off? Would he crash to the ground? Michael was about to find out.

Michael Moshier

**Michael Moshier showing how his
flying machine works**

**To learn more about flight, the
Wright brothers tested this glider in 1902.**

Michael Moshier had dreamed of flying
since he was very young. As a boy, he read
everything he could about flying. He read
an ancient Greek story about a boy named
Icarus whose father made him a pair of
wings. He also read about Orville and
Wilbur Wright, two brothers who invented
the first airplane.

In college, Michael took the kinds of
courses that would help him understand the

science of flying. After he graduated, he joined the Navy. Now Michael was flying planes every day. Yet he still had his flying dreams. They were not about flying inside a big airplane. His dreams were about flying free like a bird. Airplanes and helicopters were a fine way to get around, but Michael wished there was a simpler way. He didn't want to have to drive to the airport or buy a ticket or wait in line.

The kind of flying machine Michael dreamed of did not exist, so he decided to invent one. He knew that many people had tried to get a personal flying machine off the ground.

An early model of a helicopter

He knew, too, that there were good reasons why they had failed.

What is the difference between flying in an airplane and flying in a personal flying machine? In an airplane, you sit in a comfortable seat. There is a wall and a window between you and the engines. In a personal flying machine, the engine is strapped on your back. If Michael was going to fly, he had many problems to work out.

First, his invention needed a powerful engine. It had to be powerful enough to lift him off the ground. Michael had several engines to choose from, from electric motors to rockets. An electric motor would not work. It needed too many batteries. All those batteries would make the machine too heavy. It would never be able to get off the ground.

A rocket engine couldn't be used, either. Such an engine became too hot when flying great distances. Because the engine would be next to Michael's body, he would get burned. A rocket engine would be noisy, too. Michael needed to be able to hear what was going on around him, not just the sound of the engine.

Rocket engines

Michael tested many kinds of engines. Finally, he settled on a type of gasoline engine that worked well.

Now that Michael had his engine, he needed to create **lift** and **thrust**. Lift is the power that picks the machine up off the ground. Thrust is the extra power needed to push or pull the machine through the air.

Propellers could do both of these things, but which kind worked best? Michael wanted his flying machine to lift him straight up in the air and then carry him forward. To do this, Michael chose special propellers called ducted fans. These propellers turn round and round inside of a tube.

A ducted fan

The shape and lightweight design of the ducted fans help Michael's machine get off the ground.

To control the engine and the propellers, Michael would use his hands. One hand would work the **throttle** to make his engine run faster or slower. The other hand would control the machine's direction.

It was time for Michael to test his invention. Around him were all the people who had helped him. Other people were there who might help him pay for new and better models. That's if he could get his machine off the ground.

Michael hit the throttle and the motor picked up speed. The propellers turned faster and faster. Michael felt himself being lifted off the ground. He was flying!

On that first flight, Michael rose only 2 feet (60 centimeters), no farther than he was willing to fall. He had done what he set out to do, though. He had proven that a personal flying machine could work.

Since that first test flight, a newer model of the machine flew 60 feet (18 meters). The flight lasted about a minute.

Michael piloted the flying machine for 19 seconds.

GLOSSARY

antennae (an-TEN-ee) thin, rodlike organs used to feel things, located on the head of insects and certain other animals

cyborg a living being with mechanical parts

electrode a wire through which electricity flows

engine a machine that uses energy to run other machines

environment the natural world that surrounds us

exhaust (eg-ZAWST) smoky air made by burning gas or other fuels

germanium (jer-MAY-nee-um) a grayish white element used in electronic devices

gyroscope (JYE-ruh-skope) a spinning wheel-like object used to keep balance and direction

hardy able to survive difficult conditions

high-tech having to do with the latest technology

Ice Age a period of time about 12,000 years ago when ice and glaciers covered much of Earth

integrated circuit (IC) a tiny electronic device made up of many transistors

lift the force of air on an airplane's wings that helps it fly

obstacle (OB-stih-kuhl) something that is in the way

platform a flat surface for people to stand on

pollution anything that harms Earth's air, land, or water

propellers a set of turning blades that provides the force to move a machine through air

rubble the broken parts of a fallen building

sensitive able to see or feel small differences

silicon a natural element found in Earth's crust and used in electronic devices

technology (tek-NAH-luh-jee) work that deals with electronics and computers

throttle a device that controls an engine's speed

thrust the force that moves an object forward

transistor a small device that switches electricity on and off

unit something that is part of a larger group

FIND OUT MORE

Chipping Away
www.pbs.org/wgbh/aso/mytheory/computers
Play an on-line game and see if you can figure out which computer is ENIAC.

Robo-roach
www.ento.vt.edu/~sharov/3d/virtual.html
Create your own cyber insect at this site and see what it can do.

Make Way for Segway
www.segway.com
After you learn more about how Segway works, watch a video clip of it in action.

Flying Solo
www.trekaerospace.com
Read about the latest developments taking place in self-propelled aviation.

More Books to Read

The Computer by Gayle Worland and George Keremedjiev, Capstone Press, 2003

Into the Air: An Illustrated Timeline of Flight by Ryan Ann Hunter, National Geographic Society, 2003

Robots Rising by Carol Sonenklar, Henry Holt, 1999

What a Great Idea! Inventions that Changed the World by Steve M. Tomecek, Scholastic, 2003

INDEX

ENIAC, 5, 8-11, 13
flying machines, 5, 34, 35, 37, 38, 40-43
Gibson, Charles, 26, 28
Icarus, 36
integrated circuit (IC), 6, 13, 14
Kamen, Dean, 5, 26-30, 32
Kilby, Jack, 5, 6, 12, 13
Manchester, New Hampshire, 29
Moshier, Michael, 4, 5, 34-42

Noyce, Robert, 5, 6, 12
Philadelphia, 8
Robo-roach, 4, 5, 17-, 21-24
Segway HT, 26-33
Shimoyama, Isao, 5, 16, 18-24
University of Pennsylvania, 9
University of Tokyo, 16
Wright, Orville, 36
Wright, Wilbur, 36

PHOTO CREDITS

Cover © DigitalVision/PictureQuest
1, **16**, **21**, **22** Katsumi Kasahara/Associated Press
3, **15** PictureQuest
4 (top left), **7** Dia Max/ Taxi/ Getty Images
4 (top right), **17** Reuters
4 (bottom left), **30** Andrew Laker/Associated Press
4 (bottom right), **43** Newscom/Getty Images
6 (left) Paul Buck/Newscom
6 (right) David Breslauer/Associated Press
8 University of Pennsylvania/Associated Press
9 Glenn Mitsui/Photodisc/Getty Images
10 Francis Miller/ Time Life Pictures/Getty Images
11 Nick Koudis/Photodisc/Getty Images
12 Photo Researchers
13 Paul Buck/Newscom
14 Tom Way/ IBM/ Associated Press

18 Mike Derer/ Associated Press
19 (top), Ryan McVay/ Photodisc/Getty Images
19 (bottom), Photo Researchers
20 Clyde S. Gorsuch/ Clemson University
25 Shizuo Kambayashi/ Associated Press
26 Joel Page/ Associated Press
27 Suzanne Plunkett/ Associated Press
28 iBot/ Associated Press
29 Photodisc/Getty Images
31 Don Farrall/Photodisc/ Getty Images
33 Jacqueline Larma/ Associated Press
34 Eric Risberg/ Associated Press
35 Paul Sakuma/ Associated Press
36 Bettman/Corbis
37 Digital Vision/Getty Images
38 Associated Press
39 Maxim Marmur/ Associated Press
40, **41** Paul Sakuma/ Associated Press

MEET THE AUTHOR

The author of more than two hundred picture books, Mary Packard has been writing for children for as long as she can remember. She lives in Northport, New York, with her husband and her cat, Fraggle.

Packard read her first biography when she was in third grade. It was about a deaf and blind girl named Helen Keller. She enjoyed the book so much that she didn't stop reading until she had read every biography in the children's section of the library.

Packard believes that reading about how other people face challenges in their lives can inspire us to find new ways to cope with our own problems. It's also a fun way to try out things you might not think of doing in real life, like climbing a mountain, for instance.